This book belongs to:

Published by *The Abilities In Me*
Written by Gemma Keir
Illustrations copyright © 2020 by Adam Walker-Parker
Edited by Emma Lusty and Claire Bunyan

ISBN Paperback: 9781689559850
ISBN Hardback: 9781527247611
First printed in the United Kingdom, 2019

www.theabilitiesinme.com

The abilities in me

Save Christmas

Written by Gemma Keir
Illustrated by Adam Walker-Parker

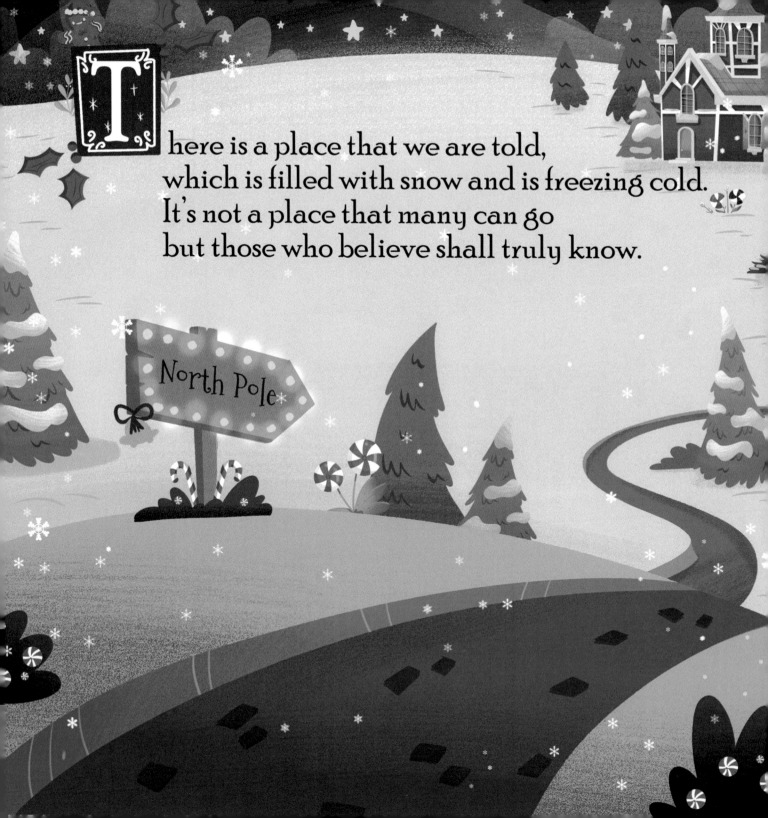

There is a place that we are told,
which is filled with snow and is freezing cold.
It's not a place that many can go
but those who believe shall truly know.

North Pole

The North Pole is the home of a man
who wears a red suit and proudly stands.
He has rosy cheeks and smiles with glee,
his name is 'Father Christmas'
and he works on Christmas Eve.

The stars shine brightly across the northern sky,
the reindeer line up as they get ready to fly.

Over in the workshop, the gifts are wrapped.
The elves prepare the sleigh and they fill up the sack.

Father Christmas sets off and
the reindeer take flight,
he must travel the world
all in one night.

He slides down the chimneys,
opens doors with magic keys

and places the
presents underneath
Christmas trees.

When he arrives at this one house,
his legs go wobbly as he sees a mouse.
He leaps into the air with his feet off the ground,
he goes flying backwards and makes a loud sound!

A little girl then wakes from her bed,
"I hear Father Christmas!" she excitedly says.
She runs down the stairs and sees something is wrong;
Father Christmas is hurt and doesn't feel strong.

She calls up her friends who know what to do...
"Christmas needs saving and it's down to you!"
A small group of children arrive at the door
and approach Father Christmas who sits on the floor.

They all have super abilities,
a gift they share inside.

They are here to save Christmas
and deliver far and wide.

Father Christmas feels worried that he's running late and is thinking of the cookies sitting out on the plates.

The children help him to get back on his feet
and call down the reindeer who fly down to the street.

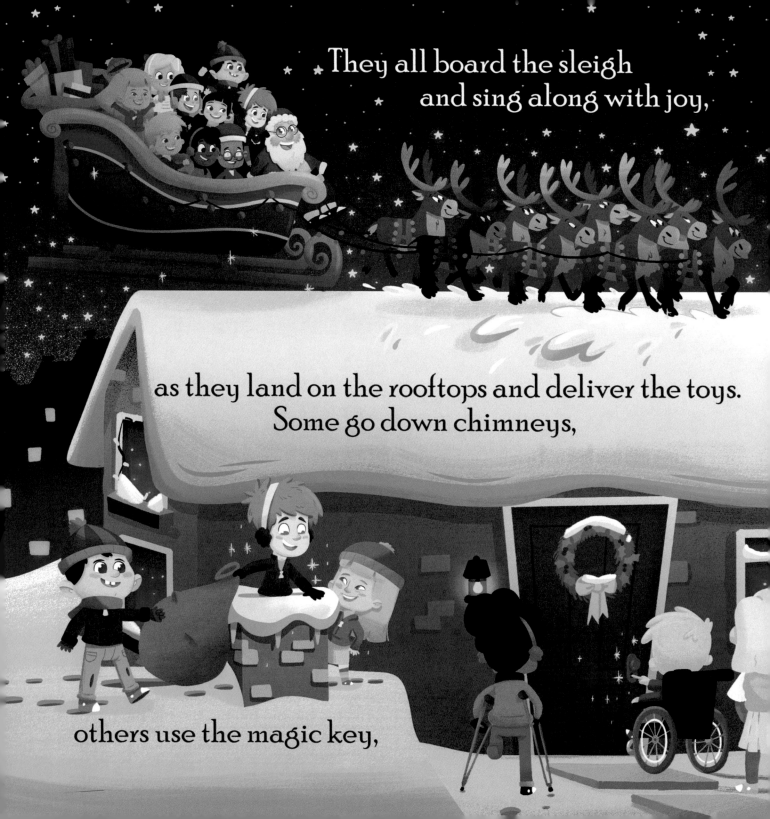

They all board the sleigh
and sing along with joy,

as they land on the rooftops and deliver the toys.
Some go down chimneys,

others use the magic key,

then they meet in a beautiful room
around a Christmas tree.

Some listen by the staircase to make sure there's no sound.
Others look around the house to make sure
no-one is found.

The little girl hands down presents,
her friends place them on the floor
They all sneak out, one by one, through the front door.

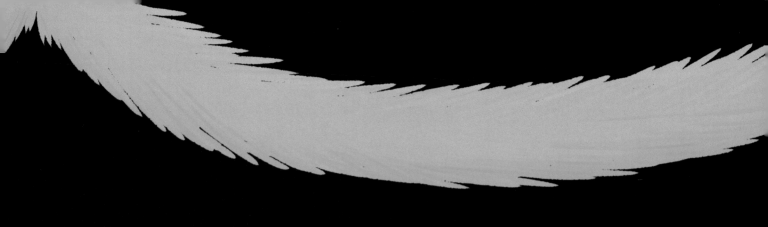

Oh no!
The milk, cookies and carrots are still on the plate.
So a little boy takes a bite and says
"This tastes great!"

They visit the last house and give the children their toys.
Father Christmas feels so happy and says to the girls and boys

"Thank you for saving Christmas and teaching me to believe, that if we all help each other we can simply achieve."

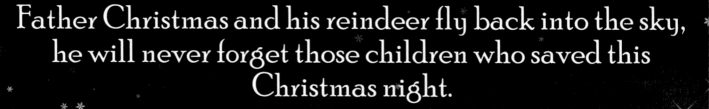

Father Christmas and his reindeer fly back into the sky, he will never forget those children who saved this Christmas night.

Merry Christmas!

Draw Father Christmas.

Write down the things that you love about Christmas:

_____

_____

_____

_____

_____

About the Author

My name is Gemma Keir, I am the book author for "The abilities in me" children's book series from Hertfordshire, England. I am a mum to a child with a range of medical conditions, including 22q Deletion who has inspired me to write these incredible stories. I am proud to have received qualifications in Special Educational Needs and Disabilities and Sensory Awareness plus specialist training in Behaviour and Safeguarding. These books provide awareness of a range of needs in children today and will be extremely popular for school settings and families who have a child with these conditions. I aim to change the whole perception of these children by promoting the abilities they do have and prevent potential bullying later in that child's life. I feel that this is possible, because children around them will be taught, from a young age and in a positive light, to have awareness and be open-minded. My vision is for children with special educational needs and disabilities to have a book to read about a character who is just like them. I aim to bring inclusivity to children's literature, acceptance and positivity.

www.theabilitiesinme.com

www.facebook.com/theabilitiesinmebookseries

About the Illustrator

My name is Adam Walker-Parker, I am a professional illustrator from Scotland. I have worked in the art industry for 12 years now, I began my career as an artist, choosing to paint figurative and wildlife paintings. I now illustrate children's books and find joy in creating something magical and inspiring for children to see.

www.awalkerparker.com

www.facebook.com/awalkerparkerillustration

www.instagram.com/awalkerparkerillustration

MORE BOOKS COMING SOON

We create children's picture books, based on characters of young children with varying disabilities. Each book will feature a child with a condition, and we aim to create a bright, colourful and positive outlook on every child with special needs. We are all unique and beautiful in every way, shape and form. This collection of books will show how each child can celebrate their abilities within their disability, find acceptance and create awareness to those around them. These books will touch the hearts of your homes, schools and hospital settings, and most importantly, your child will have a book to read, based on a special character, just like them.

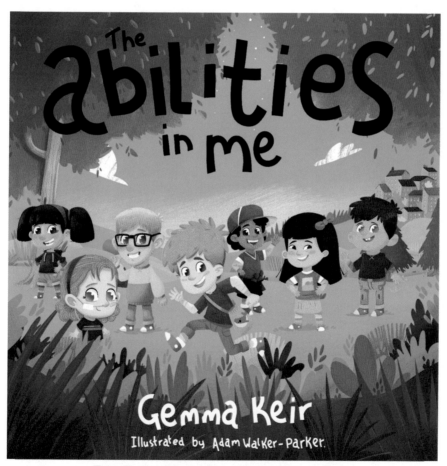

Title: The Abilities In Me - Children's Book Series
Written by Gemma Keir
Cover and Illustrations by Adam Walker-Parker

Made in the USA
Las Vegas, NV
22 October 2024

10322274R00024